WHEEL AWAY!

by **Dayle Ann Dodds**

illustrations by **Thacher Hurd**

Harper & Row, Publishers

2 3 4 5 6 7 8 9 10

Library of Congress Cataloging-in-Publication Data
Dodds, Dayle Ann.
   Wheel away!
   Summary: A runaway wheel takes a bouncy, bumpy,
amusing journey through town.
   [1. Wheels—Fiction.   2. Stories in rhyme]
I. Hurd, Thacher, ill.   II. Title.
PZ8.3.D645Wh 1989   [E]   87-27091
ISBN 0-06-021688-3
ISBN 0-06-021689-1 (lib. bdg.)

10/93 ½ Price Books, IA $ 4.00

For Glen, Jaime, and Greg
D.D.

For Manton
T.H.

Oh no! See it go!

pa-da-rump

pa-da-rump

pa-da-rump-pump-pump

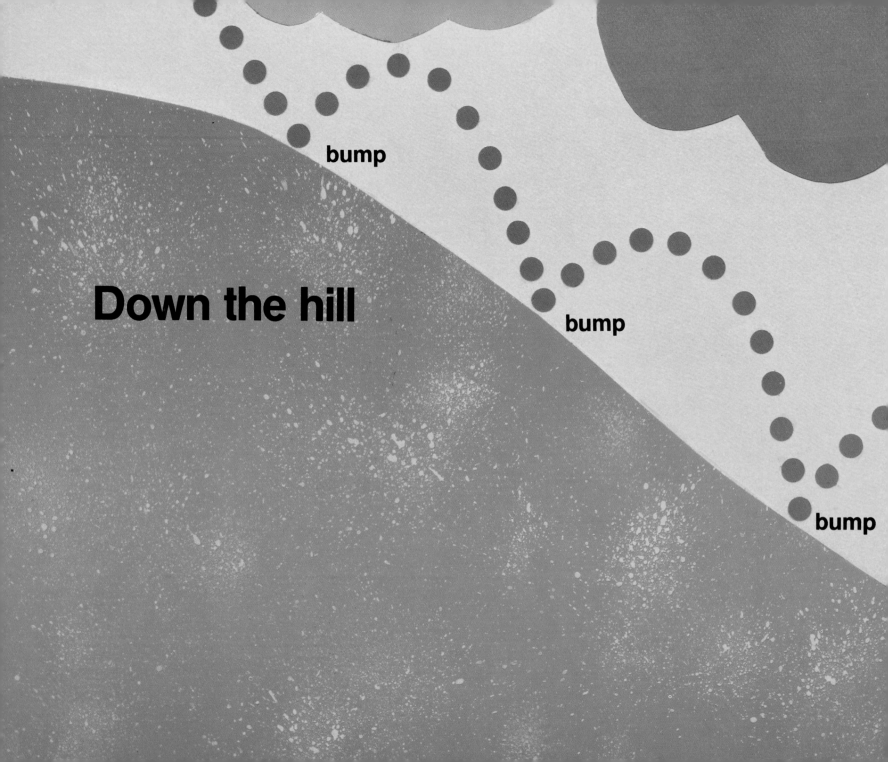

Through the mill

thump

thump

thump

In the lake

splash

splish

splish

splish

zip

zap

zip

Under the shirts

whip

whap

whip

Across the dirt

Between the pens

oink

oink

oink

On top of the hens

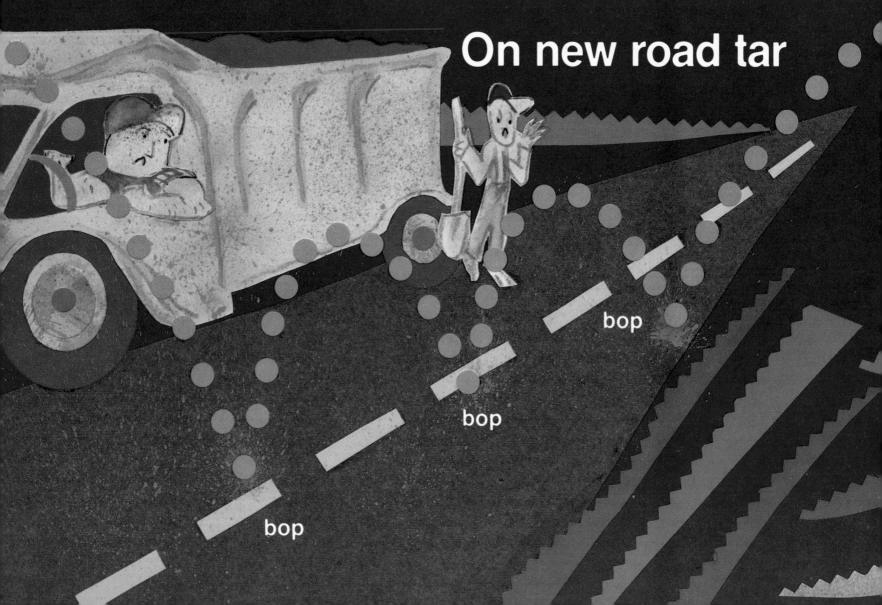

Over paint cans

squirt

squirt

squirt

Under paint man

splirt

splirt

splirt

In front of the truck

clickety-clack

In back of the duck

quackety-quack

Oh no! See it go!

pa-da-rump   pa-da-rump

pa-da-rump-pump-pump

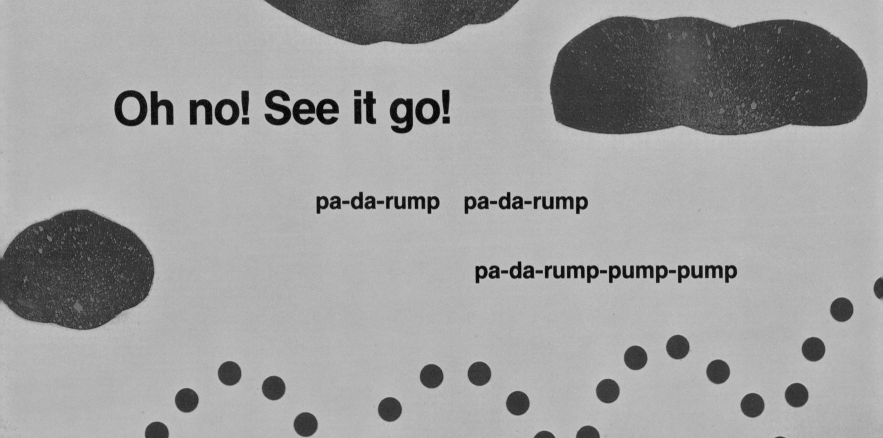

climbing

climbing climbing climbing climbing

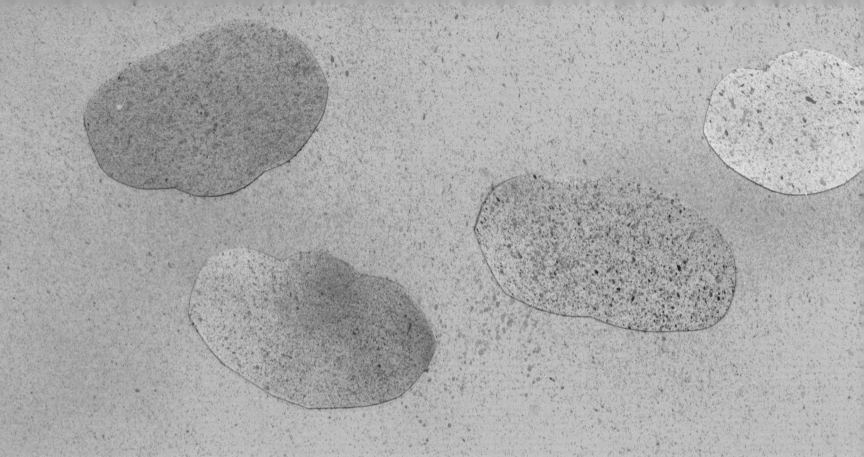

slowing

slowing slowing slowing

Oh no!

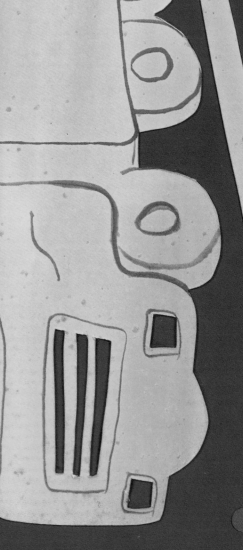

Coming back!

pa-da-rump   pa-da-rump

pa-da-rump-pump-pump

quackety-quack

clickety-clack

squirt

squirt

squirt

splirt

splirt

splirt

splirt

stop!

stop!

stop!

bop

bop

bop

bop

pa-da-rump   pa-da-rump

pa-da-rump-pump-pump

boink

boink

boink

boink

oink

oink

oink

oink

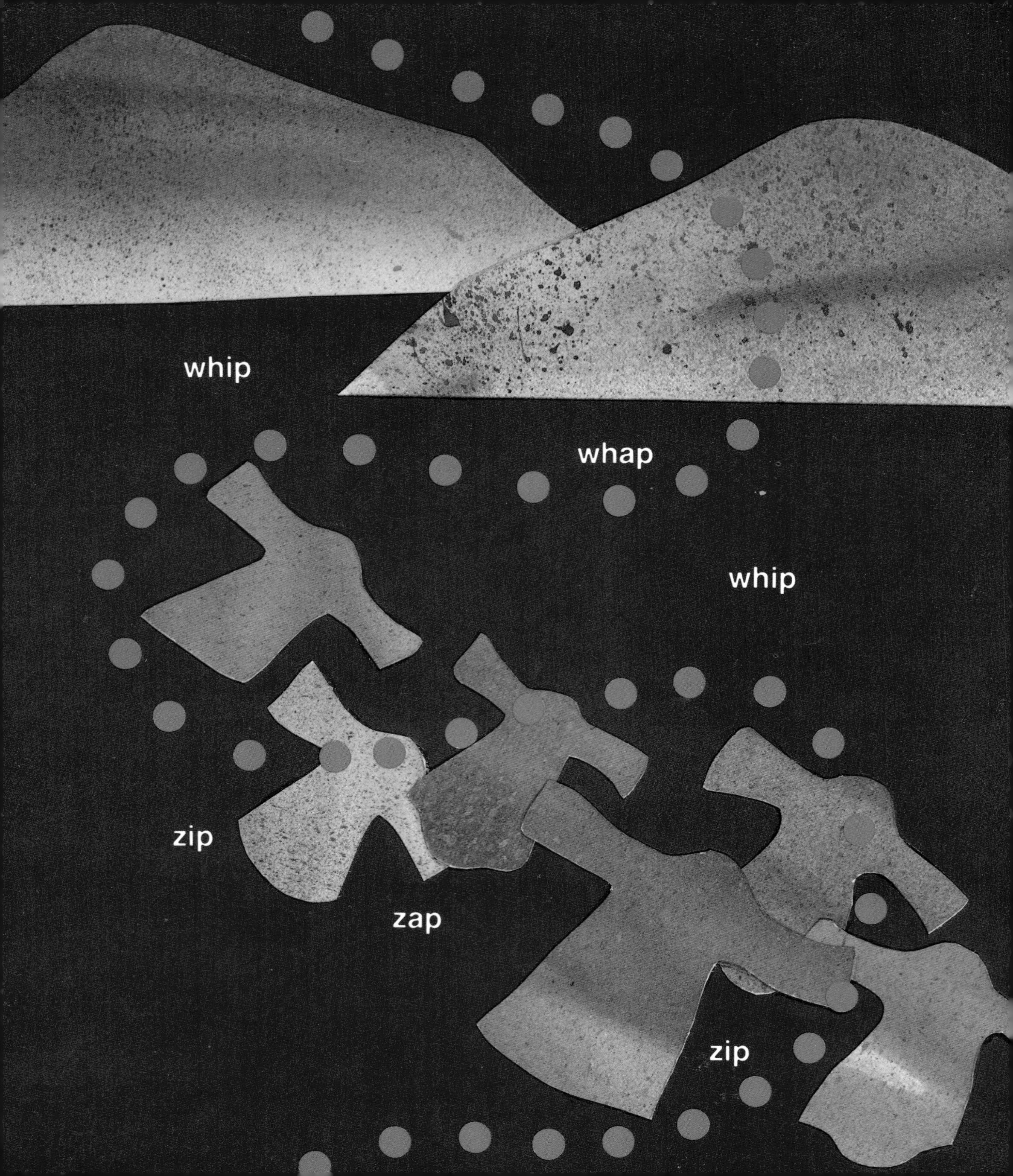

whip

whap

whip

whip

zip

zap

zip

zip

squish
squish
squash
squash
squish
squish

splish
splish
splash
splish

bump

bump

bump

bump

thump

thump

thump

climbing

climbing

climbing

climbing

slowing

slowing

slowing

slowing

back.